PRO LiNGUA LEARNING

The Grammar You Need

Level 3: Writing with Clarity and Accuracy

Mark Alves
with Eileen Cotter and Henry Caballero

Second Edition

1. Developing Descriptions & Explanations

Overview

❶ Because its courses are online,
❷ With its online courses,
❸ Offering online courses,

…the college is convenient for students.

The college's courses are online…

❹ , which makes it convenient
, making it convenient.

❺ , not in classrooms.

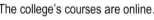

Visit *ProLinguaLearning.com* to download the **free Student Workbook** for this card and to learn about the **TGYN online learning apps**.

TGYN LEVEL 3

1.1 Adverb Clauses

Adverb clauses and other descriptors answer important questions.

What is the cause?

Since / Because courses are online, students have more flexibility.

What is the purpose?

The student took online courses so that she could work full time.

Under what conditions?

If / When courses are online, students have more flexibility.

Why is the situation unexpected or less likely?

Many students prefer classrooms although flexibility is important.

In contrast to what?

While some students prefer online courses, others do not.

Hot Tip In the sentences above, if the adverb clause comes first, we use a comma. If second, there is no comma.

However, adverb clauses with "while" are different because this word has two meanings. Use a comma before "while" to indicate *contrast* and no comma to indicate *time*.

Ali was taking the course online, while Mai was not: CONTRAST
Ali was taking the course online while he was working full time. TIME

With or without what?

Some students cannot attend college `without` online courses.

Compared to what?

`Compared to / Like / Unlike` in-person courses, online courses allow (OR do not allow) students to communicate easily.

Instead of what?

Students must compose all questions and comments in writing `instead of / rather than` communicating in person.

In order to do what?

`To save time,` some students take online courses.

Because of what?

Some students can work full time `due to / as a result of` online courses.

Despite what?

`Despite / In spite of` this flexibility, some students do not do well in online courses.

Hot Tip To add clarity, academic writers typically place commas after prepositional phrases at the beginning of sentences. **(as in this sentence)**

Why?   **When?**   **Under what condition?**
Due to working   *When she works*   *If she works*

Working full time,
she has little time to study.

Hot Tip The participial phrase always refers to the subject of the main clause.

Working full time, **she** has little time to study.

Effect

which caused / which led to / which created

causing
Clients complained, **leading to** a tense situation.
creating

Logical Conclusion

which means / which indicates / which suggests

meaning
Few bought the product, **indicating** the quality was poor.
suggesting

Definition

which is defined as / which means / which refers to

defined as
This is a hybrid course, **meaning** a combination of online and
referring to   classroom instruction.

It helps businesses

, <u>not</u> individuals.
exclusion

, <u>especially</u> local businesses.
emphasis

, <u>even</u> very small businesses.
unexpected situation

2. Making Nouns Specific and Clear

Overview

A photo

1 **Which** photo?

2 **Whose** photo?

3 A photo **of what/whom**?

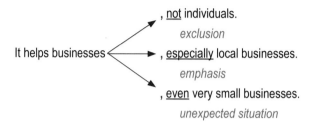

4 A photo **that shows what**?
A photo **showing what**?

5 A photo **to tell what story**?

a fam**ous** / fascinat**ing** / post**ed** photo   **ADJECTIVES**

a <u>newspaper</u> / <u>wedding</u> / <u>class</u> photo   **NOUN MODIFIERS**

Singular: the <u>journalist's</u> photo

Plural: *the <u>journalists'</u> article*

Hot Tip To show variety of expression, writers often alternate between adjective and possessive forms. This approach works well when writing about countries and religions.

<u>Adjective Form</u>	<u>Possessive Form</u>
the Mexican economy	*Mexico's economy*
Buddhist beliefs	*Buddhists' beliefs*

2.3 Prepositional Phrases

the photo **of** *Charlie Chaplin*

a film **about** *an orphan*

a study **on** *the Mexican economy*

2.4 Full and Reduced Adjective Clauses, Part II

Full Adjective Clauses

a photo **which / that** showed Chaplin in 1920…

a photo **in which** no one smiled…

the actor **who / that** won the award…

the boy **Ø / whom / who / that** Chaplin hired…

Chaplin, **whom / who** she interviewed, was well known.

Reduced Adjective Clauses after Nouns

- **"-ing" (active)**

  The woman who stars in the film also wrote it.

  ⬇

  The woman **starring** in the film also wrote it.

- **"-ed" (passive)**

  Videos **that are posted** online are often humorous.

  ⬇

  Videos **posted** online are often humorous.

Nouns as Reduced Adjective Clauses (Appositives)

That is Charlie Chaplin, **who was a famous actor and director.**

⬇

That is Charlie Chaplin, **a famous actor and director.**

2.5 Infinitive Phrases (Expressing Purpose)

a technique **which is used to add** suspense

⬇

a technique **to add** suspense

a photo **to illustrate** the 1920s

an exercise **to strengthen** the legs

Common Errors with Nouns

"-s" Endings

Add "**-s**" to plural countable nouns.

- ~~Computer is useful.~~ → Computers are useful.

  (OR **A** computer is useful.)

Do not add "-s" to uncountable nouns.

- ~~equipments~~ → equipment

"The"

Some nouns <u>always</u> need "the".

- on internet → on **the** internet

Some nouns <u>often</u> need "the".

- economy → **the** economy

"The" is typically **not** used in general statements.

- Millions of ~~the~~ people use ~~the~~ computers.

Determiner Agreement

Determiners must agree with the nouns that follow them.

- ~~this governments~~ → **this** government

  (OR **these** governments)

- ~~several instance~~ → **several** instances

Pronoun Agreement

Pronouns must agree with the nouns they represent.

- ~~If **a homework assignment** is too long, students might not finish **them**.~~ → If homework assignment**s** are too long, students might not finish **them**.

> See Appendix 2 in the free Student Workbook for a list of these nouns
>
> ProLinguaLearning.com

---

3. Making Topics Specific and Clear

Overview

① Specific Nouns to Add Clarity

- ***Historians*** are ***interpreters*** of the past.

② Gerunds to Focus on Actions

- ***Thinking*** about an event from different perspectives is important.

③ Introductory Prepositional Phrases to Add Context

- ***With respect to history***, there can be many interpretations.

④ Noun Clauses to Refer to Complex Ideas

- ***Why events happen*** can be difficult to determine.

⑤ "It is…" to Emphasize an Opinion or Observation

- ***It is*** essential for historians to be as objective as possible.

⑥ Active or Passive Voice to Reflect the Topic

- Historians ***can study*** the past in many ways.
- The past ***can be studied*** in many ways.

3.1 Selecting Specific Nouns

General	→	Specific
you/people		parents, patients, students, historians
they		the government, companies, society
a lot		almost half, a majority of, 5.3 million
Everyone knows		Research / Studies / The article shows(s)

Hot Tip Writers can also add specific details to general nouns to make them clear.

General	→	Specific
families		immigrant families, families with young children
stores		online stores, stores offering student discounts
people		educated people, people with college degrees

3.2 Focusing on Actions with Gerunds

- Using actions as subjects

  Writing research papers is a common task in history courses.

- Listing actions as examples

  *Historians do various activities, such as **teaching** and **writing**.*

- Increasing academic tone

  You must cite your sources. → **Citing sources** is required.

3.3 Adding Context with Prepositional Phrases

In terms of the causes,

Regarding the causes, } historians still disagree.

As for the causes,

3.4 Developing Complex Ideas with Noun Clauses

Why the Roman Empire fell is debated among historians.

Who discovered America first is still uncertain.

Archaeologists analyze bones to determine **how** humans have evolved.

Paleontologists use fossils to estimate **when** dinosaurs disappeared.

3.5 Stating Opinions & Observations with "It is…"

- "It is" + adjective + noun clause

  It is clear / obvious / possible / doubtful that historians will agree on the causes of Rome's fall.

- "It is" + adjective + "for" + noun + infinitive

  It is important / crucial / essential / necessary for university historians to publish their work.

- "It" + passive voice + noun clause

  It has been shown / demonstrated / proven that the Egyptian pyramids are over 4,500 years old.

3.6 Choosing Active vs. Passive Voice

- topic + active verb

  Jonas Salk <u>developed</u> the first polio vaccine in the early 1950s. } In a paragraph about Jonas Salk

- topic + passive verb

  The first polio vaccine <u>was developed</u> (by Salk) in the early 1950s. } In a paragraph about polio

Hot Tip The passive voice is…

- **frequently used for non-human subjects.**

  <u>Nobel Prizes</u> are awarded each year in Oslo, Norway.

- **frequently used with modal verbs.**

  The scientific method <u>must be used</u> by clinical researchers.

- **frequently used in common academic expressions.**

  Sociology <u>can be defined as</u> the study of human societies.

  Defining: *is defined as, is considered (to be), is known as*

  Categorizing: *are divided into, can be categorized into, is comprised of*

  Reporting: *was reported, has been shown, can be demonstrated*

  Expressing opinion: *can be prevented, must be stopped*

4. Creating Flow through Cohesion and Variety

4.1 Techniques to Create Flow

MAIN FOCUS

The pollution levels in this area are a concern for…

⬇

THIS/THAT/THESE/THOSE + SYNONYM

This contamination was the cause of…

⬇

DIFFERENT WORD FORMS

Contaminated water also leads to…

⬇

PRONOUNS

It will continue to be a problem if…

⬇

EXAMPLES OF THE TOPIC

For example, water containing certain industrial chemicals is…

⬇

KNOWN INFORMATION → NEW INFORMATION

Despite the dangers of these chemicals, politicians have not…

Hot Tip Successful writers use a variety of approaches to create a clear flow of ideas, not just basic connectors such as *however*.

4.2 Connecting Known Info to New Info

Known information: *High lead levels were found in the school's water.*

TIME CLAUSE (when, before, after, once, etc.)

When these high levels were found,

    known

    the school had to replace its water pipes.

    new

TIME WORD + -ing VERB

After replacing the pipes,

    known

    the school retested the water's lead levels.

    new

-ing PHRASE (having + past participle)

Having approved the new test results,

    known

    the school allowed students to drink the water again.

    new

CONTRAST PHRASE (despite, in spite of, even with, etc.)

Even with the new pipes,

    known

    some students were still nervous about the water.

    new

Hot Tip Writers often use perfect tenses (present and past) to introduce background information (known information).

*Once the pipes **had been replaced**, the water became safe.*

    known info   new info

4.3 Placement of Academic Connector Words

NO EXTRA EMPHASIS

In 1960, U.S. cars emitted large quantities of pollutants. *However,* *by 2010, the quantities had decreased by 98%.*

EMPHASIZES THE TIME PHRASE

In 1960, U.S. cars emitted large quantities of pollutants. *By 2010, however,* *the quantities had decreased by over 98%.*

EMPHASIZES THE SUBJECT

Gasoline-powered cars still pollute the air. *Electric cars, in contrast,* *have little or no carbon footprint.*

Connectors which can be moved for emphasis:

• however	• for example	• as a result
• in contrast	• for instance	• moreover
• on the other hand	• therefore	• furthermore

---

5. Expressing Facts, Viewpoints, Predictions & Imagined Situations

5.1 Expressing Facts & Viewpoints

Facts

…cannot be argued. They tend to be detailed and specific.

Example:

In 2021, the average person consumed 21.4 kg of sugar.

  Date   Specific Detail   Statistic

Hot Tip In academic writing, facts are usually expressed with simple tenses (simple present/past tenses), NOT continuous tenses.

Viewpoints

…are arguable. They are evaluations, judgments, or recommendations.

Example:

It appears that sugar may pose a significant health risk,

  Evaluation Verb   Evaluation Adjective

so people should clearly eat less of it.

     Modal Verb   Evaluation Adverb

Common Evaluation Verbs and Patterns	Common Evaluation Adjectives and Adverbs
appear, seem, should, might	*important, major, minor*
be clear/likely/evident that…	*clearly, probably, possibly*

Hot Tip Avoid overgeneralizations. *(All Americans?)*

~~*Americans*~~ *consume too much sugar.*

Many Americans *consume too much sugar.* ✔

Often inaccurate	Often more accurate
all	many, a majority of, a large number of
none	a minority, few, a small number
always	frequently, typically, generally
never	rarely, seldom, typically/generally do not
X is…	X tends to be…, X is often…, X can be…

5.2 Expressing Predictions & Imagined Situations

Predictions

…are guesses about the future based on available information.

Example:

If global production does not increase, sugar

  "If Clause (present tense)   *prices will probably rise.*

                   Modal Verb   Prediction Adverb

Common Modal Verbs for Predictions	Common Adverbs for Predictions
could, may, might, will	*likely, possibly, probably*

Imagined situations

…are not real. They are guesses about what could be true (in the present or future) or what might have been true (in the past) under different circumstances.

Present / Future

Many people would likely eat less sugar if they knew the dangers.

Modal Verb   Prediction Adverb   "If" Clause (past tense)

Past

Sugar might not have become so popular if ways to crystallize it had not been developed in India over 1,600 years ago.

Modal Verb   "If" Clause (past perfect tense)

Common Modal Verbs for Imagined Situations
would, could, might

Hot Tip For imagined situations, accurate verb tenses are essential to express ideas clearly.

For Present or Future Meaning

modal + base verb in the result clause

Many people might eat less sugar

simple past tense in the "if" clause

…if they knew the dangers.

For Past Meaning

modal + have + past participle in the result clause

The demand for honey might have risen

past perfect tense in the "if" clause

if crystallized sugar had not been available.

---

6. Citing Sources and Using Information

6.1 Acknowledging Sources

Introductory Phrases

According to the Journal of Marketing Research,

Based on recent data,

As indicated/shown/stated in a 2016 study,

  } …restaurant customers order 39% more calories if the lighting is dark.

Reporting Verbs

Dr. Brian Wansink **states**, "The best diet is the one you don't know you're on."   QUOTE

Dr. Brian Wansink **asserts** that successful diets should not be overly difficult.   PARAPHRASE

Hot Tip **Tips for Reporting Information from Other Sources**

• If you do not use quotation marks, you must paraphrase (use your own words).

• In academic writing, reporting verbs are commonly used in the simple present tense.

   • The verb tense in the reported information should match the time of the event/action.

• Wansink **writes** that people live longer today.

• Wansink **writes** that life expectancy in 1900 was 49 years.

Sentence-final References

People tend to eat more if their plate is larger (**Wansink 454**).

                                    last name   *page*

6.2 Using Numbers to Support Ideas

Type	Function	Sample
Precise numbers	For charts, lists, or scientific writing	*The rate of obesity among American adults is 36.5% (CDC).*
Generalized numbers	For reporting data	*The CDC reports that over one-third of Americans adults were obese in 2017 (CDC).*
Numbers used to express opinions	For supporting a position	*The rate of obesity among American adults (36.5%) is surprisingly high.*

Hot Tip **Use numbers to support ideas.**

• Numbers may be used as interesting introductory facts or background information.

• When writers use numbers as supporting details, they usually provide an explanation or interpretation of those numbers.

The Grammar You Need, 2nd Edition

Michael Berman
Series Editor

Level 1: Building Sentences
978-0-86647-572-3
Level 2: Developing Details
978-0-86647-573-0
Level 3: Writing with Clarity and Accuracy
978-0-86647-574-7

For free student workbooks and information about our TGYN online learning apps, visit

TheGrammarYouNeed.com

or **ProLinguaLearning.com**

Pro Lingua Learning, LLC
P.O. Box 4467
Rockville, MD 20849
Office: 301-424-8900
Orders: 800-888-4741
info@ProLinguaLearning.com
Printed in the USA

ISBN 978-0-86-647574-7

PRO LINGUA LEARNING

9 780866 475747

90000 >